my
New York
garden

a gardener's journal

Liz Ball

COOL
SPRINGS
PRESS

ISBN 1-930604-10-6

NOTE: The ideas expressed in this book are not, in all cases, exact quotations, as some have been edited to fit the format. In all cases, the publisher has attempted to maintain the speaker's original intent. Further, in some cases, source materials for this book were obtained from secondary sources, primarily print media and the Internet. While every effort has been made to ensure the accuracy of these sources, accuracy cannot be guaranteed. To notify us of any corrections or clarifications, please contact Cool Springs Press.

Cool Springs Press, Inc.
112 Second Avenue North
Franklin, TN 37064

First Printing 2000
Printed in the United States of America
10 9 8 7 6 5 4 3 2 1

Design by:	Sheri Ferguson
Illustrations by:	Allison Starcher
Editorial Consultant:	Erica Glasener

Visit the Cool Springs Press website at www.coolspringspress.com

my New York garden

a gardener's journal

this is my

New York

garden

_____

name

_____

year

why keep a garden journal ?

Welcome! We New York State gardeners are known for our enthusiasm and persistence. We realize gardening is a constant learning process. We have minds of our own—and sometimes it seems that our plants do too. That's why you need *My New York Garden: A Gardener's Journal.*

Keeping a garden journal will help you keep track of how your garden grows. You will discover which plants thrive, which ones struggle, and best of all, you will discover many surprises. More than just record keeping, journaling is a way to trace your growth as a gardener. Writing down your favorite moments in the garden may help you decide which plants to add or which to replace. How does your garden make you feel? You may discover you prefer one season to another. Maybe your style of gardening has changed. A journal will help you track the evolution of your garden.

As gardeners know, weather is a huge factor in plant performance. By keeping track of air temperature, the amount of rainfall, and drastic changes (storms or droughts), we can see which plants survived and plan better for next year.

Has the environment in your garden changed? Trees and shrubs that were once small may have matured and created a shadier garden. Keeping a list of what you plant, where and when you plant it, and the source of the plant will provide useful information for the future.

Further, keeping up with what's blooming when, and how long it blooms is another reason to write daily or weekly in your garden journal. You might be surprised at how many times during the year your garden features beautiful blooms, colorful foliage, or fantastic fruits. Some of the best color combinations happen by accident and remembering which plant blooms and when it blooms from year to year is not easy. With good journal records, you may recreate pleasing plant combinations and avoid repeating mistakes.

How often you fertilize, prune, and water are other things to keep track of in your garden journal. Which techniques have been most successful? If you have a particular pest or disease problem with one plant, what methods were effective in eradicating or controlling the problem? If your roses were beautiful last year, when did you prune them and how much did you prune? When did you divide your daylilies and where did you plant the different kinds of spring bulbs? All of these questions can be answered in the pages of *My New York Garden*.

getting started with your garden journal

By keeping daily records, you can check your journal and chart your most successful garden practices. Whether it's how and when you propagated a favorite perennial, when the clematis first came into bloom, or when you noticed the scent of a particular narcissus, your New York garden journal will provide the ideal format for keeping in touch with your garden and what it can teach you. Here's how to begin.

- Designate a day and a time during the week to write in your journal. You might discover that early morning coffee time or the end of the day works best.
- Use a favorite pen and keep it with your journal. Write brief, clear notes (*rainy and cool with temp around 60° F, Phlox 'David' has been in bloom for 2 weeks, Butterfly bush still loaded with flower buds, planted two hardy geraniums in perennial garden, 'Johnson's Blue' and 'Claridge Druce', purchased from the specialty nursery in Oregon*).
- Keep a 5"x 7" envelope tucked in the back of your journal to hold photographs and pictures from catalogs or magazines that inspire you. Be sure to identify and label pictures.
- List existing trees, shrubs, perennials, and bulbs and include a sketch of where they are located. This will be especially helpful over the years when you make changes in your garden.

    Once you get used to journaling, you may find that you look forward to writing about your garden as much as you enjoy adding new plants.

G rowing plants has been always been part of life in New York in spite of its considerable variation in geography and climate. Distinctive because its boundaries touch both the Great Lakes and the Atlantic Ocean, New York State boasts the great natural advantages of numerous lakes and rivers, rugged forested mountains, and flat, fertile plains. Its range of latitude and altitude offers a diverse ecology that supports opportunities for all kinds of gardening.

The topography of New York State is dominated by the Allegheny Plateau. Layered above the plateau is the Erie-Ontario Plain and Mohawk Valley, its narrow finger lakes intruding into the plateau below.   In the east, the Adirondack Mountains rise to meet New England. Below them, the Hudson Valley stretches south to New York City with Long Island extending like a punctuation mark below it.

While climate varies over these regions, it is mostly because of changes in elevation. The contrasts are greatest in winter, when temperatures flirt with freezing on coastal Long Island but dip dramatically below it upstate. To the west, the Great Lakes moderate the weather somewhat. Gardeners benefit from reliable snow cover in most areas which protects both soil and plants. Summer temperatures are much more uniform throughout the state.

In the system of cold hardiness zones developed and defined by the USDA, parts of New York State range from zones 7 through 4. These zone designations are based on the average annual minimum temperature of an area, each zone number indicating a difference of 10°F. The lower the number, the colder the winters. Knowing which zone you live in is a helpful guide to choosing and caring for plants that overwinter outdoors.

choosing plants

There are so many choices that it is often difficult to decide which ones to select for your yard and garden. Start by eliminating those that are not labeled for your area's hardiness zone. Although every home landscape has unique features that create warmer or more sheltered areas—micro-climates where less hardy plants may do well—it is a good idea to start with the official zones as guidelines for perennial plants that must survive winter. Later, as you observe the seasons, prevailing airflow, sunlight, and moisture patterns, experiment with some marginally hardy plants.

There are several other issues that influence the choice of plants for most homeowners. One is the desire for diversity. Not only is a variety of types and kinds of plants more attractive, it also creates a healthier overall environment. Lots of different plants support lots of beneficial creatures to carry out pollination and pest control. The more plant species, the better the balance of pest and predator. A related issue is wildlife habitat. As suburban development fragments the New York wilderness and deprives wildlife of food and shelter, backyards can help replace them. Choose plants that bear berries, cones, and seeds for birds and other small mammals. Plants that are native to New York do the best job. Another issue is choosing plants for a practical purpose such as screening out noise or a view, blocking winter wind to save on heating bills, or preventing soil erosion on a steep hill. Perhaps you want plants that are fragrant or good for shearing as hedges or for cut flowers. If all these factors make choosing plants too overwhelming, consider hiring a professional landscape designer to help you analyze your property, soil, and goals.

preparing for plants

After choosing a site that offers the right sun or shade, the most important thing you can do for your plants is to give them good soil. Since most soil in New York is somewhat acidic, a pH test is likely to confirm that it is fine for most plants. An inexpensive pH meter with a probe that you stick into the soil will register any major deviation from the desirable range of 5.5 to 7.0. Chances are, though, that the soil may be a bit too acidic for the lawn. That's why homeowners routinely spread lime on lawns in the fall every couple of years to "sweeten" the soil for northern turfgrasses.

It provides calcium too, which all plants need.

It is hard to know by looking at soil whether it is nutritious or fertile. It is very important to know if the major nutrients, nitrogen (N), phosphorus (P) and potassium (K) are not only present, but present in the right proportion. The best way to determine this information is with a soil test done by a laboratory. Kits for the test are available from your county Agricultural Extension office. Instructions are enclosed. Test results mailed to you will indicate things like amounts of nutrients, existing nutrient deficiencies, pH imbalance and how to correct them.

Handling your soil is the best way to determine its texture. The best soil both drains well and retains moisture because it has lots of spongy humus in it. Improve thin or clay soil by mixing in organic matter in the form of homemade or municipal compost, peat moss, or chopped leaves. Spread a thin layer as a topdressing on the lawn to improve soil under the turf. Periodically, core aerate the lawn and dig in established beds to reduce compaction and introduce air into the soil. The oxygen supports essential microbial life, worms, and other natural residents that process nutrients for plants.

keeping your plants happy

The key is to success with plants is to keep them happy — supplying nutritious, aerated soil, sufficient moisture, appropriate light, and support if needed. If they are not stressed, they can handle most insect and disease problems. Sometimes a change in their environment such as drought, the removal of a tree that gave shade, or pollution of some sort unavoidably compromises their health. You may correct the situation by moving the plant or watering. Occasionally, environmental stress also triggers a population explosion of some pest which overwhelms the vulnerable plant. It may be necessary to pinch or hose off the bugs or spot spray an insecticide on them to reduce the infestation until the plant recovers. Here are some basics for keeping plants happy.

fertilizing

Over the years, even the most fertile soil is depleted of nutrients if
organic matter is not regularly added. This is particularly true where
plants must constantly produce flowers, seeds or fruits for harvest and in
lawns where plants must constantly regenerate their foliage due to
repeated mowing. Provide consistent, uniform nutrition to your home
landscape by using a general purpose, slow-acting, granular fertilizer
at the beginning of the growing season. Whether it is organic or synthe-
sized, its nitrogen (N), phosphorus (P) and
potassium (K) will remain available to
plant roots. If your soil test
reveals an imbalance of these
major nutrients, then
temporarily use a product
which features a greater
proportion of the one you
need. This is indicated
on the label in words and
by a series of three numbers
indicating the ratio of N, P and K.
Avoid overfertilizing plants indoors
or outside. Insects and diseases
love the excessive tender new growth that a
rich diet promotes.

watering

New York State has historically enjoyed generous moisture. However, in
recent years, weather patterns have changed everywhere, and droughty
periods during the summer and fall have occurred intermittently. The
best insurance against prolonged drought is to install a drip irrigation
system in beds planted with shrubs, trees, ornamental, and food plants.
It delivers water most efficiently and effectively for healthier plants and
water conservation. Standard hose sprinklers are fine for lawns during
brief drought periods. During longer droughts it is less stressful for
northern grasses to go completely dormant than to be intermittently

watered. Most outdoor plants will need about 1 inch of water per week, whether from rainfall or irrigation. Plants in containers in the sun need more water, especially in the summer.

mulching

Spread a 2- or 3-inch layer of some organic material such as chopped leaves, pine needles, or commercial bark product over all the bare soil under and between plants on your property. This is how nature protects and renews the soil in the wild. In planted beds, organic mulch discourages weeds and helps the soil retain moisture. As it decomposes in the hot weather, it contributes humus and microbial life to the soil to keep it healthy. Stubborn perennial weeds may require hand or mechanical pulling or a spot treatment with a safe soap or glysophate-based herbicide. As the mulch layer becomes thin over the season, add more, but never pile it up against plant stems. In the winter, mulch insulates soil to protect it from alternate freezing and thawing which disturbs plants, especially bulbs.

grooming

Supervise the development of your plants to keep them sturdy and healthy. Thin young ones if they become too crowded. Guide their growth and shape by erecting supports for those that threaten to flop in wind or rain. Keeping certain flowers and vegetables off of the ground protects them from disease and provides them with better light and air circulation. Some plants, such as impatiens, basil, and chrysanthemums benefit from pinching back stems to make them more compact. Others, such as tomatoes, form stronger stems and larger fruit or flowers if subsidiary branchlets, called suckers, are routinely clipped off. Removing faded flowers before they form seeds, called deadheading, promotes continued blooming for lots of flowering annuals, as well as some perennials. Proper pruning of woody vines, trees, and shrubs improves their access to light and air, stimulates their growth, helps them heal properly, and prevents disease and insect problems.

New York Garden Favorites

Here is a list of plants that are easy to grow, readily available, adaptable to various growing conditions in New York State, and which help provide year-round interest. These plants can be very beneficial to your New York garden because they provide brilliant color, some attract birds and wildlife, and most require minimal maintenance. Give these a try!

Annuals

- Begonia, Wax Leaf — *Begonia semperflorens-cultorum* hybrids
- Coleus — *Solenostemon scutellarioides* hybrids
- Cosmos — *Cosmos bipinnatus*
- Geranium — *Pelargonium* x *hortorum*
- Impatiens — *Impatiens wallerana*
- Marigold — *Tagetes* hybrids
- Pansy — *Viola* x *wittrockiana*
- Petunia — *Petunia* x *hybrida*
- Snapdragon — *Antirrhinum majus*
- Sunflower — *Helianthus annuus*

Perennials

- Astilbe — *Astilbe* x *arendsii*
- Black-Eyed Susan — *Rudbeckia*
- Chrysanthemum, Garden — *Chrysanthemum* x *morifolium*
- Daylily — *Hemerocallis* hybrids
- Goldenrod — *Solidago* hybrids
- Lamb's Ear — *Stachys byzantina*
- Lenten Rose — *Helleborus orientalis*
- Michaelmas Daisy — *Aster novi-belgi*
- Plantain Lily — *Hosta*
- Threadleaf coreopsis — *Coreopsis verticillata*

Bulbs

- Canna — *Canna* x *generalis*
- Crocosmia — *Crocosmia masoniorum*
- Crocus — *Crocus* spp.
- Daffodil — *Narcissus* spp.
- Dahlia — *Dahlia pinnata*
- Flowering Onion — *Allium* species
- Grape Hyacinth — *Muscari armeniacum*
- Iris, Bearded — *Iris germanica*
- Lily — *Lilium* species
- Tulips — *Tulipa* spp.

Seaside favorites

- Bayberry — *Myrica pensylvanica*
- Bigleaf Hydrangea — *Hydrangea macrophylla*
- Black Gum — *Nyssa sylvatica*
- Clematis — *Clematis paniculata*
- Common Privet — *Ligustrum vulgare*
- Firethorn — *Pyracantha coccinea* 'Lalandei'
- Little Bluestem — *Schizachyrium scoparium*
- Rock Cotoneaster — *Cotoneaster horizontalis*
- Rugosa Rose — *Rosa rugosa*

Ground covers

- Bugleweed — *Ajuga reptans*
- Blue Fescue — *Festuca ovina*
- Creeping Juniper — *Juniperus horizontalis* 'Bar Harbor'
- Creeping Phlox — *Phlox subulata*
- Deer Fern — *Blechnum spicant*
- Lady Fern — *Athyrium filix-femina*
- Pachysandra — *Pachysandra terminalis*
- Periwinkle, Common — *Vinca minor*

Lawn grasses

- Kentucky Bluegrass — *Poa pratensis*
- Perennial Ryegrass — *Lolium perenne*
- Tall Fescue — *Festuca elatior*

Roses

- Floribunda Rose — *Rosa* 'The Fairy'
- Landscape Rose — *Rosa* spp.

Trees

- American Beech — *Fagus grandifolia*
- Ginkgo — *Ginkgo biloba*
- Littleleaf Greenspire® Linden — *Tilia cordata*
- Red Buckeye — *Aesculus pavia*
- Red Maple — *Acer ruburm*
- Red Oak — *Quercus rubra*
- Sugar Maple — *Acer saccharum*
- Weeping Willow — *Salix alba*

Small flowering trees

- Crabapple — *Malus* spp.
- Eastern Redbud — *Cercis canadensis*
- Flowering Dogwood — *Cornus florida* or *Cornus kousa*
- Japanese Pagodatree — *Sophora japonica*
- Japanese Stewartia — *Stewartia pseudocamellia*
- Smoketree — *Cotinus coggygria*
- Weeping Higan Cherry — *Prunus subhirtella* 'Pendula'

Evergreen trees:

- American Holly — *Ilex opaca*
- Atlas Cedar — *Cedrus atlantica*
- Eastern White Pine — *Pinus strobus*
- Norway Spruce — *Picea abies*
- Hinoki False Cypress — *Chamaecyprais obtusa* 'Gracilis'
- Leyland Cypress — *Cupressocyparis leylandii*

Flowering shrubs

- Azalea — *Rhododendron*
- Beautybush — *Kolkwitzia amabilis*
- Butterfly Bush — *Buddleia davidii*
- Common Lilac — *Syringa vulgaris*
- Forsythia 'Spectabilis' — *Forsythia* x *intermedia*
- Glossy Abelia — *Abelia grandiflora*
- Japanese Andromeda — *Pieris japonica*
- Mountain Laurel — *Kalmia latifolia*
- Rhododendron — *Rhododendron* spp.
- Spirea 'Anthony Waterer' — *Spirea* x *bumalda* 'Anthony Waterer'
- Viburnum — *Viburnum* x *burkwoodii*

City decks, patios and small space gardens:

- Bird's Nest Spruce — *Pices abies* 'Nidiformis'
- Boston Ivy — *Parthenocissus tricuspidata* 'Veitchii'
- Crapemyrtle — *Lagerstroemia indica*
- Dwarf Alberta Spruce — *Picea glauca* 'Conica'
- Japanese Acuba — *Acuba japonica*
- Japanese Maple — *Acer palmatum*
- Young's Weeping Birch — *Betula pendula* 'Youngii'

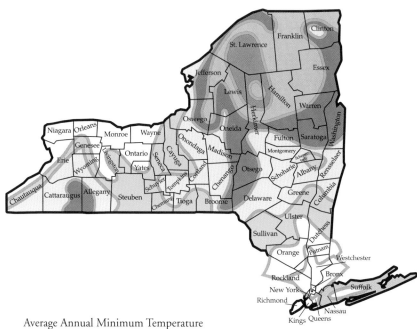

Average Annual Minimum Temperature

Zone	Temperature
2A	-45° F to -50° F
2B	-40° F to -45° F
3A	-35° F to -40° F
3B	-30° F to -35° F
4A	-25° F to -30° F
4B	-20° F to -25° F
5A	-15° F to -20° F
5B	-10° F to -15° F
6A	-5° F to -10° F
6B	0° F to -5° F
7A	5° F to 0° F

To create a
little flower is the
labour of ages.

— *William Blake*

January

garden observations

_____
_____
_____
_____
_____
_____
_____

what's the weather like?

_____
_____
_____
_____
_____
_____

Start the year off right! Photograph your garden at least once every month. This will help you with your planning and planting schemes.

what have I planted/transplanted?

_____
_____
_____
_____
_____

garden notes

What is a weed? A plant whose virtues have not yet been dicovered.

—Ralph Waldo Emerson

January

garden observations

Order seeds now for
your favorite annuals,
perennials and vegeta-
bles. Cut out color
photographs and create
your own record for
what you order.

what's the weather like?

When planning your
garden, use a large
sheet of graph paper
with 1/4 inch grids.
A scale of 1 inch
= 4 feet is a useful
proportion.

what have I planted/transplanted?

garden notes

january | week 2

January

garden observations

_____

_____

_____

_____

_____

what's the weather like?

_____

_____

_____

what have I planted/transplanted?

_____

_____

_____

_____

_____

_____

garden notes

Check house plants for signs of insects and disease. Spots, speckles or webs on leaves indicate pests are present.

january week 4

January

garden observations

what's the weather like?

Tip to Remember:
You may also use
vegetables as
ornamental plants.
Ornamental peppers
and sweet potato vine
selections are good
examples.

what have I planted/transplanted?

garden notes

February

garden observations

_____

_____

_____

_____

_____

_____

what's the weather like?

_____

_____

_____

_____

_____

Take a walk through
your garden, and
plan additions to
create winter interest
for next year.

what have I planted/transplanted?

_____

_____

Did You Know?
The only tulip color
that has not yet been
developed is any
shade of blue.

_____

_____

_____

garden notes

february | week 1

february | week 2

February

garden observations

what's the weather like?

When in doubt, call your local Extension Service. Master Gardeners there will provide information (and the advice is free!)

what have I planted/transplanted?

garden notes

february | week 3

February

garden observations

Extend the life of
your cut flowers.
Remove the lower
leaves and re-cut the
stems before
arranging them in
lukewarm water.

what's the weather like?

what have I planted/transplanted?

garden notes

Though I do not believe
that a plant will spring
up where no seed has been,
I have great faith in a
seed. Convince me that
you have a seed there,
and I am prepared to
expect wonders.

— Henry David Thoreau

february | week 4

February

garden observations

what's the weather like?

Tip to Remember:
Fill clear plastic
milk jugs with
water and place
around young
tomato plants.
They will provide
warmth overnight
for young plants,
helping you get a
jump on spring.

what have I planted/transplanted?

garden notes

march | week 1

March

what's blooming?

_____

_____

_____

_____

_____

Direct sow wildflower
seeds where you want
them to grow in
climates with USDA
zones 1 through 6.
(Check the zone map
in the introduction to
identify your zone.)

what's the weather like?

_____

_____

_____

_____

_____

Take a soil test now
so you will know how
to prepare your garden
for the next season.

what have I planted/transplanted?

_____

_____

_____

_____

_____

garden notes

march week 2

March

what's blooming?

_____

_____

_____

_____

_____

Tip to Remember:
Plan to add a few
annuals to your
perennial garden
to help provide
season-long blooms.

what's the weather like?

_____

_____

_____

_____

Watch for aphids on
shrubs as they leaf out.
Treat with insecticidal
soap or any other
labeled pesticide,
if needed.

what have I planted/transplanted?

_____

_____

_____

Start tomato seeds for
transplants 4-6 weeks
before optimum plant-
ing time in your area.

_____

garden notes

march | week 3

March

what's blooming?

Single-flower forms of marigolds and zinnias are more appealing to butterflies than the double-flower forms.

what's the weather like?

Did You Know? Viburnum is a member of the honeysuckle family.

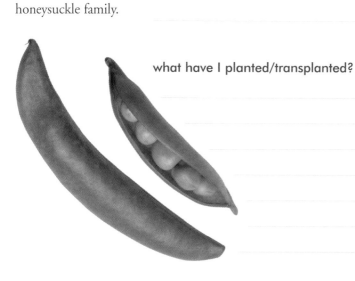

what have I planted/transplanted?

garden notes

March

what's blooming?

what's the weather like?

Hummingbirds love
tubular flowers such
as trumpet vine, coral
honeysuckle, and
nicotiana. Plant lots
of these if you want to
attract hummingbirds.

what have I planted/transplanted?

garden notes

*Half the interest of a
garden is the constant
exercise of the imagination.*

— C.W. Earle

a p r i l | w e e k 1

what's blooming?

what's the weather like?

Have you
photographed
your garden lately?
This will help with
your garden planning
and design ideas.

what have I planted/transplanted?

An easy time to weed
is the day after a
gentle rain, when the
soil is slightly moist,
and weeds are easy to
pull—roots and all.

4-7-19
Planted daffodils on side of road
Mulched leaves on flower gardens
Furtilized flower gardens

april | week 2

what's blooming?

Propagate some
of your favorite
broadleaf shrubs using
this simple layering
technique: Select a
branch that is close to
the ground. Bend the
branch so that it is in
contact with the soil.
Cover the branch
with soil. Water well
and hold the branch
in place with a brick.
In six weeks, check to
see if there are roots.
Once the roots are
firmly established,
cut the new plant
off from the
mother plant.

what's the weather like?

what have I planted/transplanted?

*As is the gardener, such
is the garden.*

— Hebrew Proverb

a p r i l week 3

what's blooming?

Crocus have come & gone

Tip to Remember:
When digging a hole
for a tree, it's best to
dig the hole at least
half again as wide as
the size of the rootball
(much wider is even
better). Use the same
soil you dug out to
backfill around
the rootball and
water-in well.

what's the weather like?

50°, damp, cool nights 30-40°

Turn your compost
pile. If you haven't
started one already,
call your Extension
Service for advice.

what have I planted/transplanted?

april week 4

what's blooming?

what's the weather like?

Wooden clothespins
can be used as plant
markers.

Place grow-thru stakes
above plants that need
support in early
spring, and in a
short time they will
cover the stakes.

what have I planted/transplanted?

may week 1

May

Plan to prune back spring-blooming azaleas and other shrubs such as forsythia or spirea after they finish flowering. This way you won't cut off any potential flower buds for next year.

Check plants once or twice a week for insect and disease problems. It's easier to control a small infestation if it's discovered early.

what's blooming?

what's the weather like?

what have I planted/transplanted?

garden notes

may | week 1

may week 2

what's blooming?

_____

_____

_____

_____

_____

_____

what's the weather like?

_____

_____

_____

_____

Incorporate a slow-release fertilizer in the soil of hanging baskets and container plantings. This will provide nutrients for several months in one application.

what have I planted/transplanted?

_____

_____

_____

_____

_____

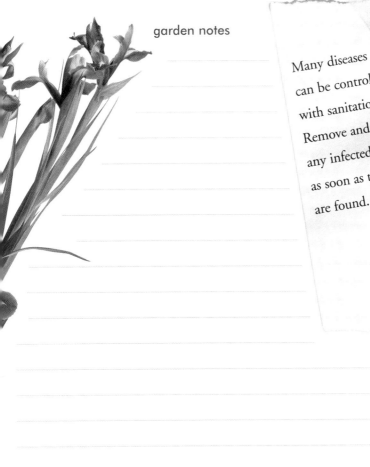

garden notes

Many diseases
can be controlled
with sanitation.
Remove and destroy
any infected leaves
as soon as they
are found.

may | week 2

may week 3

what's blooming?

Parsley and fennel
provide food for
butterfly caterpillars.

what's the weather like?

Interest children
in gardening by
planning a small
child's garden. A
bean tee-pee is fun
to plant and grow!

what have I planted/transplanted?

garden notes

The best time for slug hunting is at night using a flashlight and a pair of gloves.

may week 4

May

what's blooming?

what's the weather like?

what have I planted/transplanted?

garden notes

Tickle it with a hoe and it will laugh into a harvest.

— English Proverb

june | week 1

June

what's blooming?

A perennial garden looks wonderful when planted against a background of a wall, a hedge, or evergreen shrubs.

what's the weather like?

A plant's scientific name consists of a genus and an epithet. The genus and the epithet are always italicized and the genus begins with a capital letter. A third word in the name may refer to a specific variety, called a cultivar. It is set off by single quotation marks.

what have I planted/transplanted?

garden notes

what's blooming?

Use vines to create
vertical interest in the
garden. If you don't
have a wall or fence
on which to train
them, a lattice or
arbor will work.

what's the weather like?

You can create
your own portable
seep irrigation
system by punch-
ing a few holes in
plastic containers
and placing them
beside plants that
need additional
moisture.

what have I planted/transplanted?

garden notes

*Though an old man,
I am but a young
gardener...*

— Thomas Jefferson

june | week 3

June

Plan to shear fall-blooming asters to make them bushier and more compact.

what's blooming?

what's the weather like?

Did You Know?
Even though a plant may be identified as self-cleaning, flowers are better off if you deadhead, or remove the spent blooms as often as you can. This will allow the plant to use its energy to make more flowers and leaves instead of making seeds.

what have I planted/transplanted?

garden notes

june week 4

what's blooming?

what's the weather like?

BTK (*Bacillus thuringiensis kurstaki*) is an organic biological control that is effective against many caterpillars and is safe to use on vegetable crops. *Bacillus thuringiensis* 'San Diego' is effective against some leafeating beetles.

what have I planted/transplanted?

garden notes

july | week 1

Harvest herbs for drying as soon as they come into flower. Bundle them up with a rubber band and hang them on a line in a dark, dry place with good air circulation. To preserve the best flavor once they are dry, store the herbs in airtight containers away from heat and light.

Press some flowers and add to this journal. It's a pretty record of what you planted.

what's blooming?

what's the weather like?

what have I planted/transplanted?

garden notes

july week 2

what's blooming?

what's the weather like?

what have I planted/transplanted?

Deadhead hybrid tea roses throughout the summer to encourage more blooms.

garden notes

july week 3

what's blooming?

what's the weather like?

Most unwanted
summer heat comes
through east- and west-
facing windows, not
through well-insulated
roofs and walls. Plant a
deciduous tree for shade.

what have I planted/transplanted?

garden notes

july | week 4

what's blooming?

Plants use calcium to build strong cell walls and stems. Deficiencies can cause blossom-end rot on tomatoes.

what's the weather like?

Did You Know? The Greeks and Romans used lavender in bath water. In fact, the Latin name "lavare" means, "wash".

Tip to Remember: When planting seeds, position them in geometric patterns so that you will be able to distinguish them more easily from weed seedlings.

what have I planted/transplanted?

garden notes

Gardening is the purest
of human pleasures.

— Francis Bacon

august week 1

what's blooming?

what's the weather like?

Preserve basil leaves
by mixing them in
the blender with a
small amount of
water. Fill ice cube
trays with the mix-
ture. Once they
freeze, put them in
freezer bags. This way
you will have basil
to use in your favorite
Italian dishes all
winter long.

what have I planted/transplanted?

garden notes

august week 2

August

what's blooming?

For the best selection, order your spring-flowering bulbs or purchase them locally when they become available in your area. Keep them cool and dry until you plant them.

what's the weather like?

Take some photographs of your garden to refer to later when planning for next year.

what have I planted/transplanted?

garden notes

August

If you haven't already done so, draw a plan of your property showing existing trees and shrubs in relation to your house. Make notes throughout the year indicating those areas that receive full sun, shade or a mix of sun and shade. This will help you to choose the right plant for the right place.

what's blooming?

what's the weather like?

what have I planted/transplanted?

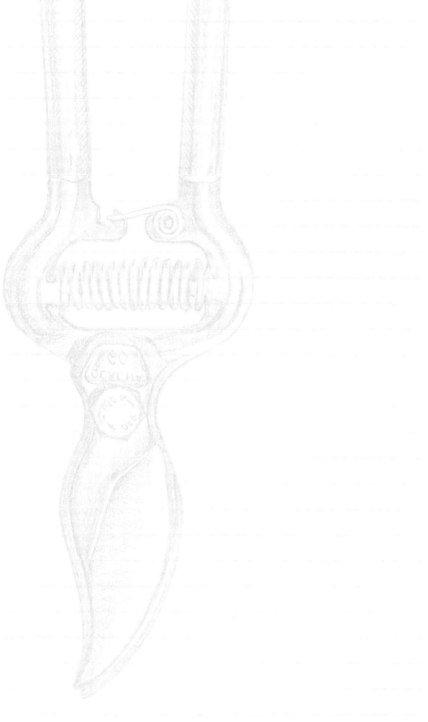

August

what's blooming?

Water your compost
pile when the weather
has been dry.

what's the weather like?

Order three or four
types of paperwhite
narcissus to force at
two-week intervals.
You will have flowers
from Halloween into
the New Year!

what have I planted/transplanted?

Continue to harvest
vegetables as soon as
they are ripe. Regular
harvesting increases
production.

garden notes

He who plants a garden plants happiness.

—Chinese Proverb

september | week 1

what's blooming?

what's the weather like?

Expand your plant
collection by exchang-
ing seeds and plants
with fellow gardeners.

what have I planted/transplanted?

Add some shrubs to
your garden that will
offer winter interest
such as colorful bark,
or unusual shapes.

garden notes

september | week 1

september

what's blooming?

what's the weather like?

If you haven't
started one
already, begin
a compost pile
and let it
overwinter.
In six months
you should
have "black
gold" to mix
into your
garden.

what have I planted/transplanted?

garden notes

The frost hurts not weeds.

— Thomas Fuller

september

what's blooming?

what's the weather like?

what have I planted/transplanted?

If your annuals are beginning to look ragged, pull them and replace with some mums, pansies, or flowering kale.

september | week 4

september

what's blooming?

Use dried seed
heads such as sedum
and lotus for fall
decorations.

Visit your favorite
nursery to select a tree
or shrub for that spot
in the garden that
needs something new.

what's the weather like?

what have I planted/transplanted?

garden notes

september | week 4

october | week 1

what's blooming?

what's the weather like?

Plant a tree in honor
of a birth or in
memory of a
loved one.

Fall leaf color is trig-
gered by cooler tem-
peratures, shorter
days, and less light.

what have I planted/transplanted?

garden notes

October

what's blooming?

what's the weather like?

what have I planted/transplanted?

garden notes

Sprinkle annual
rye grass seed on
top of the soil
of pots you are
forcing. By the
time the bulbs
bloom, it will
create a green carpet
underneath them.

october | week 3

October

what's blooming?

what's the weather like?

Tip to Remember:
Parsley is a good
plant for bed edges.
It also looks great
grown in containers
with pansies.

what have I planted/transplanted?

Use golf tees to mark
areas where bulbs are
planted.

*Heaven is under our feet
as well as over our heads.*

— Henry David Thoreau

october | week 4

October

what's blooming?

what's the weather like?

Did You Know?
The word 'wort',
as in St. John's Wort,
is an old English
term that means
"medicinal plant".

what have I planted/transplanted?

garden notes

tending my garden

october | week 4

november | week 1

what's blooming?

what's the weather like?

Fall is the best time
to direct sow wild-
flower seeds in
USDA zones 7-9.
(Check the map in
the introduction to
verify your zone.)

what have I planted/transplanted?

garden notes

Autumn is a second spring when every leaf is a flower. —Albert Camus

november | week 2

November

what's blooming?

what's the weather like?

Continue to mow
your lawn for as long
as it keeps growing.

Clean and sharpen
garden tools. Lightly
coat with oil to
prevent rust.

what have I planted/transplanted?

garden notes

November

what's blooming?

what's the weather like?

what have I planted/transplanted?

garden notes

Extend the life of
your fresh-cut holiday
tree by storing it in a
cool shady place until
you move it indoors.
Re-cut the trunk
before moving it
indoors and use
plenty of fresh water
in the reservoir.

november | week 4

what's blooming?

For best results, store
unused seeds in a
cool, dark place in
an air- and water-
resistant container.

what's the weather like?

Selecting the right
tool for the job can
prevent most injuries.
Wear safety gear
when operating
power equipment.

what have I planted/transplanted?

garden notes

december week 1

December

garden observations

Make a wreath for
the holidays. Rose
hips, bittersweet, and
euonymus are good
choices for materials.

what's the weather like?

what have I planted/
transplanted?

garden notes

A garden is a friend
you can visit any time.

—unknown

december | week 2

December

garden observations

Cast iron plant,
Chinese evergreen,
heartleaf philoden-
dron, and snake plant
will tolerate low-light
conditions.

what's the weather like?

Tip to Remember:
The winter sun
provides the most
solar heat through
south-facing
windows. Avoid
planting shade trees
or evergreens that
may shade these
heat-absorbing
windows if you
need the extra
warmth.

what have I planted/transplanted?

garden notes

december | week 2

december | week 3

December

garden observations

Recycle your holiday
tree. The branches
can be removed and
used as mulch. Or
you can leave the
tree intact and use it
as a windbreak and
shelter for birds.

what's the weather like?

Don't put wood
ashes in your com-
post pile; they will
alter the pH level
too much.

what have I planted/transplanted?

garden notes

december | week 3

december | week 4

December

garden observations

what's the weather like?

what have I planted/transplanted?

garden notes

Pruning large trees,
especially those located
near utilities should
be performed by a
professional. Call a
certified arborist if you
need trees pruned.

plant inventory/history

name

when planted

where planted

size

source

price

name

when planted

where planted

size

source

price

name

when planted

where planted

size

source

price

name

when planted

where planted

size

source

price

name

when planted

where planted

size

source

price

name

when planted

where planted

size

source

price

name

when planted

where planted

size

source

price

name

when planted

where planted

size

source

price

name

when planted

where planted

size

source

price

name

when planted

where planted

size

source

price

name

when planted

where planted

size

source

price

name

when planted

where planted

size

source

price

name

when planted

where planted

size

source

price

name

when planted

where planted

size

source

price

name

when planted

where planted

size

source

price

name

when planted

where planted

size

source

price

plant inventory/history

name

when planted

where planted

size

source

price

name

when planted

where planted

size

source

price

name

when planted

where planted

size

source

price

name

when planted

where planted

size

source

price

name

when planted

where planted

size

source

price

name

when planted

where planted

size

source

price

name

when planted

where planted

size

source

price

name

when planted

where planted

size

source

price

name	**name**
when planted	when planted
where planted	where planted
size	size
source	source
price	price
name	**name**
when planted	when planted
where planted	where planted
size	size
source	source
price	price
name	**name**
when planted	when planted
where planted	where planted
size	size
source	source
price	price
name	**name**
when planted	when planted
where planted	where planted
size	size
source	source
price	price

plant inventory/history

name

when planted

where planted

size

source

price

name

when planted

where planted

size

source

price

name

when planted

where planted

size

source

price

name

when planted

where planted

size

source

price

name

when planted

where planted

size

source

price

name

when planted

where planted

size

source

price

name

when planted

where planted

size

source

price

name

when planted

where planted

size

source

price

name

when planted

where planted

size

source

price

name

when planted

where planted

size

source

price

name

when planted

where planted

size

source

price

name

when planted

where planted

size

source

price

name

when planted

where planted

size

source

price

name

when planted

where planted

size

source

price

name

when planted

where planted

size

source

price

name

when planted

where planted

size

source

price

plant inventory/history

name	name
when planted	when planted
where planted	where planted
size	size
source	source
price	price

name | name

when planted | when planted

where planted | where planted

size | size

source | source

price | price

name | name

when planted | when planted

where planted | where planted

size | size

source | source

price | price

name | name

when planted | when planted

where planted | where planted

size | size

source | source

price | price

name

when planted

where planted

size

source

price

name

when planted

where planted

size

source

price

name

when planted

where planted

size

source

price

name

when planted

where planted

size

source

price

name

when planted

where planted

size

source

price

name

when planted

where planted

size

source

price

name

when planted

where planted

size

source

price

name

when planted

where planted

size

source

price

my garden plan

suppliers & resources

photos